The Tutor's Handbook

MATH

Grade 2

Written by Carolyn Ross Tomlin

Illustrated by George Ulrich

Editor: Kathleen Hex
Introduction: Carol Wright
Book Design: Rita Hudson
Cover Design: Riley Wilkinson
Graphic Artist: Randy Shinsato
Cover Photos: Anthony Nex Photography

FS122130 The Tutor's Handbook: Math Grade 2
All rights reserved—Printed in the U.S.A.
23740 Hawthorne Blvd., Torrance, CA 90505

TABLE OF CONTENTS

As a tutor for a young child, consider your role as that of a coach. Picture the coaches you have seen running along the sidelines at local soccer games. They believe in their teams. They encourage, support, advise, and challenge to help their teams achieve victory. As a tutor, you will assume a similar role as you help the child achieve success in second grade math activities.

Patience

Probably one of the most important qualities in a coach or tutor is patience. You have a clear understanding of the math concepts that you will be helping the child develop. However, the student will not master these skills overnight. Allow the child sufficient time to explore, practice, and develop each skill you present.

Enthusiasm

Just like an athletic coach, the tutor must convey to the student a belief in his or her ability to master the skills. Be an encourager! Call attention to the progress that the child is making in math. Your sincere praise will help the child feel comfortable with taking risks and may help him or her develop confidence with math activities.

Process

Soccer coaches are obviously focused on helping their teams win. If you look closely, you will notice that coaches actually spend much of the time helping the team learn how to win a game.

As you help the student develop a variety of math strategies, try to focus a significant amount of energy on the things that the child is doing to solve the problems. Encourage the student to talk out loud as he or she thinks about and works on a problem. Pose thoughtful questions about the process used to solve a problem. This is more helpful than simply marking answers right or wrong.

Be enthusiastic about learning!

Make it a common practice to ask the child to tell you how he or she got an answer to a problem. If you discover that the child began solving an addition problem in the tens place, ask the child why he or she started there. Just as the athletic coach does not allow the team to practice over and over the wrong way to play, help the student succeed by talking about the process that will help him or her reach the correct answer. Resist the temptation to simply tell your student the correct answer, as this will result in little long-term learning. Pose questions about the problem that will challenge the child to explore and use all of the different strategies that he or she is developing. When the child correctly solves a problem, encourage him or her to describe the process used to solve it. Ask the child to reiterate the steps used to arrive at the correct answer.

In your important role of tutor as coach, have patience with your student! Remember that the child is learning as fast as he or she can. Be enthusiastic about learning! Your excitement and encouragement may help the child improve his or her attitude toward math. Finally, focus on the process of learning! It is just as important as getting the right answer.

The following grade level expectations are based on national math standards as set by the National Council of Teachers of Mathematics.

NUMBERS AND COMPUTATION

Second graders should be able to

- understand and practice place value to 1,000

- order and compare whole numbers by using the greater than and less than symbols (> and <)

- add and subtract whole numbers up to three digits

- understand and use inverse operations for addition and subtraction (7 + 8 = 15, 15 − 8 = 7)

- estimate and use mental math

- multiply by two, five, and ten

- recognize, name, and compare simple fractions

- add and subtract money amounts

- use the decimal point, dollar sign, and cents symbol

GEOMETRY

Second graders should be able to

- identify and describe two-dimensional figures (circle, square, rectangle, triangle)

- identify and describe three-dimensional figures (sphere, pyramid, cube, rectangular prism, cone)

- classify figures by shape and number of faces, edges, and vertices

- recognize congruent shapes (same size and shape)

- put shapes together or take shapes apart to form new shapes (two triangles form a square)

PATTERNS

Second graders should be able to

- identify, create, and extend geometric and number patterns

- use the 1–100 number chart

- skip count by two, five, and ten

- recognize and create fact families (3 + 4 = 7, 4 + 3 = 7, 7 − 4 = 3, 7 − 3 = 4)

DATA ANALYSIS, STATISTICS, AND PROBABILITY

Second graders should be able to

- collect, organize, and display data in bar graphs and pictographs
- use tables, graphs, and charts to evaluate data
- ask and answer simple questions about a graph or chart
- determine whether an event is more or less likely to occur

MEASUREMENT

Second graders should be able to

- use standard and nonstandard units of measurement
- recognize and understand U.S. customary and metric units for mass/weight, temperature, length, volume, capacity
- estimate and accurately measure objects
- measure lengths to the nearest inch or centimeter
- tell time to the nearest five minutes
- understand relationships of time (minutes in an hour, days in a month, weeks in a year)
- understand elapsed time in hours
- use a calendar

PROBLEM SOLVING

Second graders should be able to

- develop a variety of problem solving strategies
- use models or draw a picture to solve a problem
- choose the correct operation to solve a problem
- use manipulatives to solve a problem
- sort and classify information in a problem
- identify a pattern to help solve a problem
- determine what information is necessary or unnecessary to solve a problem
- support thinking with objects, words, or pictures

Assess Skills

As you begin working with the child, determine his or her strengths and weaknesses in a given area. Give the child the pretest provided for each section. His or her performance on the pretest will help you determine appropriate areas for skill development. Try to determine the child's level of competence by asking questions. What word might be used to show subtraction? How do we show multiplication?

Helpful Hint: Collect all necessary materials before the session begins. Children will lose interest if the tutor has to search for supplies.

Take cues from the child to determine pacing. Children acquire skills at very different rates. Keep this in mind when planning the sessions. Some concepts may require more instruction or reinforcement.

Review Concepts

Begin each session with a review of concepts previously taught. Ask questions that allow the child to demonstrate his or her understanding of the content. Try to let the student to do most of the talking, encouraging him or her to explain his or her

reasoning. Listening to the child reveals significant information about the mathematical concepts that he or she is developing. Practice with two or three problems that the child is surely capable of answering. This technique will give the student the confidence needed to master new material.

If the child has completed assignments since the previous session, review the work with him or her. Avoid the temptation to merely mark all of the problems right or wrong. Talk with the student about how the work was completed and review information as needed. Working from a wrong answer to the correct answer frequently results in a more thorough understanding of the math concept. Consider asking, "What made you think that?" or "How did you get that answer?" for correct answers as well as for wrong answers. The student will get in the habit of scrutinizing answers and reflecting on his or her thinking.

Introduce New Concepts

Introduce new concepts to be covered during the session. Whenever possible, provide concrete objects such as beans, toothpicks, or cotton balls for the child to use while working. These hands-on experiences help the child fully understand the concept and prepares him or her for exploring abstract mathematical principles. When solving the problems you present, the child should be encouraged to talk out loud to enable you to assess his or her understanding of the concept. As much as possible, connect these ideas to the child's world and show him or her how mastering math strategies will be useful.

Helpful Hint: Use the correct vocabulary as you help the child learn new concepts. In later grades, using appropriate mathematical vocabulary is very important.

Practice Makes Perfect

Practice is a very important component of any tutoring session. Provide a few problems for the child to practice, but be careful that the practice is not mindless and repetitive. This book provides a number of practice pages, but they are in no way exhaustive. Use them as guides to help you create additional problems to make sure that the student thoroughly understands the concepts.

Give careful thought to the practice you provide. Make sure that the practice requires the student to think and to apply the concepts. Once the child has demonstrated mastery, be careful not to assume he or she knows the skill. Instead, provide regular opportunities for the child to review prior concepts and practice current ones in a thoughtful, meaningful manner.

Ending the Session

If appropriate, give the child an assignment to complete independently before the next session. It is often helpful to have the child explain how he or she will complete the assigned problems before ending the session. The practice you provide will not extend and challenge the child's mathematical understanding if he or she is unsure how to proceed.

Before ending the session, make sure that the child has the necessary tools to complete the work. Pencils, paper, a multiplication chart, a 1-100 number chart, and a box of counting beans will help ensure success. Finally, review the session with the child. Have him or her explain to you the concepts learned and the process or strategies used during the session. End the session on a positive and encouraging note. Answer any questions the student may have before sending him or her off.

Tutoring in Small Groups

If you are tutoring more than one child at a time, observe how these children work in a group setting. Note the individual strengths of each child as well as the group dynamics. Does one child seem to continually dominate the discussions and answer first? Is one child particularly shy? Is anyone easily distracted by the other children? If this is the case, it might be more beneficial for that child to have an individual tutoring session.

Each student should receive some degree of individual attention from you during the tutoring session. Teach the children appropriate session behavior: wait your turn, be patient, respect the other students, give only positive remarks, help one another when you can. Encourage each child to use his or her strengths to help others.

> **Helpful Hint:** See each child as an individual with his or her own strengths, talents, and interests.

Learning Styles Make a Difference

Every child has a learning style with which he or she is most comfortable. As a tutor you should become aware of what works best for the child. Is she able to grasp the concept more easily when she reads the material? Does he need to see a visual representation of the material—a picture or a diagram? A combination of two or more methods is usually best and will vary from student to student. If you use a variety of styles, the child will learn math in ways that fit his or her learning style.

The following are some ways in which children learn:

- Auditory—learning through hearing; using music to hear a sound
- Kinesthetic—learning through doing, movement, or performing
- Linguistic—learning through the written word
- Logical/mathematical—learning through reasoning and organized problem solving, presenting events in sequential order
- Social/cooperative—learning through working with others
- Visual/spatial—learning through seeing; forming relationships

For more information on learning styles consult Howard Gardner's book *Frames of Mind* (Basic Books, 1993).

Manipulatives

Use hands-on materials to keep young minds interested. Collect items such as bottle caps, nature items (sea shells, large seeds), colored wooden beads, buttons, keys, paper clips, and rubber bands. If you travel for tutoring sessions, use plastic zip bags, empty coffee cans, or disposable plastic containers to keep manipulatives organized.

> **Helpful Hint:** Using cloth place mats or a table cloth will reduce noise when using manipulatives.

Estimation Madness

Estimate everything! For example, empty a package of dry beans into a transparent container such as a jar. Ask the child to estimate how many beans are in the container. How many cups of water are in a large pitcher? How many jelly beans are in a package? How many cereal rings are in the bowl? In this activity, it is more important to guess closely than to get the exact number.

Graphs Galore

Use data from every day situations to make graphs. Explain that picture graphs and bar graphs represent numbers that record, sort, count, and interpret data. Use a graph whenever the child presents an interesting situation, such as what he or she ate (food groups), what kinds of toys, or what kinds of clothes he or she wears. Vary between horizontal to vertical graphs so that the child learns to read and interpret all types. Present the same graph in two versions.

> **Helpful Hint:**
> Offer sincere praise. Try to be specific and praise work or behavior. Use phrases such as "You know your addition facts!" "You are showing great improvement on counting!" Use stickers as simple rewards.

Go Outdoors

Children love to get away from pencil and paper activities and go outside. On the sidewalk, make a number line or hopscotch squares for skip counting. Arrange a life-size pictograph, using stuffed animals. Have the student practice measuring capacity by filling cups with sand. Children have wonderful imaginations! Let the child create his or her own games involving math.

Calendar Fun

A large wall calendar can be used for many activities.

- Point to a date. Ask the child to tell the date in 3 more days; 5 more days.

- Ask the student, "What is your favorite day of the week?" "Why?" Have the student draw a picture of something he or she may do on this day.

- Have the student look at the calendar and skip count by two, three, four, or five from the date of a special event (such as a birthday or a vacation).

- Have the student add the numbers in a three month period. Ask, "Do all months have the same numbers?" "Do all the months have the same totals?" "Why or why not?"

- Have the student write the ordinal numbers for each day of the month. For example, January 1 is the 1st; January 2 is the 2nd.

Student Survey

Ask the child to answer the questions on the survey to the best of his or her ability. This should be as stress-free as possible. Help the student if necessary. After the survey is complete, pose open-ended questions that will encourage the child to discuss the answers. Often, other questions will arise during the discussion. Ask as many questions as necessary to gain insight into the child. This is an excellent opportunity for you to establish rapport with the student and to make him or her feel comfortable. Make the discussion nonthreatening and friendly. Keep it positive, but also try to determine the areas where the child needs work.

> **Helpful Hint:** Use this discussion time to find out about the child's interests. Using these interests during instruction and practice will help motivate and keep the child interested.

Student Survey

Read each statement. Complete the statement or circle the answer.

1 How do you feel when you do math?

_____

- -

_____

- -

_____

2 How good are you at math?

not very good   ok   very good

3 I use math everyday.

true   not true

4 Put a ✔ next to your favorite subject in school.
Put an X next to the subject you like the least.

___English   ___Social Studies
___Math   ___Spelling
___Physical Education   ___Reading

5 When I do math I like to -
_____

6 I want to improve my math grades this year.

yes   no

10
reproducible

Science/Health

To connect science and math, have the student search the weather section of a newspaper or watch the television weather broadcast for the daily highs and lows in his or her city for a one-week period. Help the child find the difference between the high temperature and the low temperature for each day. Which day had the greatest difference? Which had the least? Try this with an almanac and by checking other cities.

Math and health studies are easily connected. Make a checklist of a wide variety of foods. Have the child check off the foods that he or she consumes over a one-week period each time the food is eaten. Help the child organize the data and make a graph showing the number of foods from each food group (meat, milk or dairy products, fruits, vegetables, grains). Which food group was consumed the most? The least?

Helpful Hint: Encourage parents to become involved in their child's tutoring. Send home activities that the student can do with the family.

Language Arts

Introduce language arts to math by helping the child make a journal for future math activities. Guide the child in deciding how many pages will be needed for a 10-page book if he or she uses large sheets of paper folded in half. Ask the child to explain how he or she arrived at the number of pages needed. Allow the child to design a decorative cover. Since this is a math journal, how would you illustrate the cover? Help the student punch holes about one-half inch from the left edge and use yarn to bind the journal.

Encourage the child to use his or her journal for drawing geometric objects and shapes seen while riding in the car or walking down the street. Have the student look for stop signs, billboards, wheels, and other objects that are distinct geometric shapes. Show the student how to record the date and where the shape was seen. Finally, ask the student to draw the shape, then describe it with words.

Provide several children's books or short stories for the child to read. Ask the child to select a book and read it silently. *I Know an Old Lady Who Swallowed a Fly* by Nadine Wescott (Lothrop, 1989) would be an excellent start. Then, have the child retell the story to you by listing the events in order as they happened. What happened first? What happened second? This activity provides practice in sequencing—an important math skill. If reading is difficult for the child, use a picture book or ask him or her to make up a story.

Art

Incorporate art by helping the student make a collage. Ask the child to collect a variety of small items—buttons, sea shells, feathers, twigs, pieces of yarn, small leaves or flowers, dried beans, etc. When the child brings the items to the session, help him or her count the items and separate them. Help the child create a tally chart of the items. Then graph the data. A bar graph or pictograph would probably work best. Finally, the child can carefully glue the items randomly on a piece of construction paper to create a beautiful collage.

Social Studies

Connect math and geography through travel. Using the travel section of the newspaper (or brochures from a travel agency) and a map, help the child plan a trip to the destination of his or her choice. Help the child locate the destination on the map. Is it near or far away? Show the child how to use the map key and legend to determine how many miles away it is. How much would transportation cost? Is it more economical to travel by plane, bus, car, or boat? What sights would the child choose to see? How much would activities cost? Help the child add up the total cost of the trip.

Math All Around Us

Help the student recognize math in the grocery store. Have the student practice selecting and weighing various items from the produce section. Have him or her estimate the weight then place the items on the scale. How close was the estimate? If you purchase 2 pounds of fresh fish at $3.00 per pound, how much will you pay? Three

Helpful Hint: Get parent permission before taking the child on a field trip or eating any foods.

pounds of bananas at $.40 per pound? The grocery store is also a great place to practice identifying geometric shapes and patterns. Ask the child to identify a rectangular prism or a sphere. What is the object? Can you find a pattern in the cereal aisle?

Check the newspaper for a time schedule for local movie theaters. Have the child select a movie he or she would like to see. Most theaters offer matinees at a reduced price. What would it cost the child and a group of friends to go see a movie in the afternoon before 5:00 p.m.? How much after 6:00 p.m.? How much money should the child bring if he or she also wanted to buy popcorn?

Practice telling time with the child. Make a chart showing the events in daily life, such as the time for getting up in the morning, eating breakfast, going to school, eating lunch, playing sports, doing homework, eating dinner, taking a bath, and going to bed. Use a large teaching clock with moveable hands for the child to explore and set the hour and minute hands. Help the child find the elapsed time between these activities. If you started school at 8:00 a.m. and finished at 3:00 p.m., how long were you at school?

CONCEPTS SECOND GRADERS SHOULD KNOW

- place value to 1,000
- adding and subtracting up to three-digit numbers
- estimating
- ordering and comparing whole numbers
- multiplying by 2, 5, 10
- recognizing, naming, and comparing simple fractions
- adding and subtracting money
- inverse operations

Activities

1. Read the children's counting poem "Over in the Meadow" (Simon & Schuster, 1986). As you read, have the child count out the correct number of counting beans or tokens that correspond to the animals in the poem. Ask the child to illustrate his or her favorite animal or insect and the number with crayons and paper.

2. Play a game of dominoes. Use store-bought dominoes or help the child make his or her own with index cards. Place two dominos together and have the child add the numbers. Use the inverse operation (subtraction) to check by taking away a domino.

3. After reading the story *Stone Soup* by John Warren Stewig (Holiday House, 1991), make a pot of soup. Count the number of carrots, potatoes, onions, and other vegetables as they are added to the soup. Add the totals. Extend the activity by having the student make a pictograph or a bar graph showing the number of each vegetable. Which vegetable was used most? Bon appetit!

4. Using sidewalk chalk, draw a number line on the ground outside. Call out a number for the child to stand on (3). Start with that number and create an addition problem (3 + 2). The child hops forward that many spaces (2 spaces), repeats the problem (3 + 2) and supplies an answer (3 + 2 = 5). Try the same procedure for subtraction, with the child jumping backward on the number line.

5. Ask the child to check the contents in an all-purpose kitchen drawer or miscellaneous items in a shoebox. Ask the child to group the items and record the number. How many rubber bands, paper clips, pens, and pieces of scratch paper? Pose questions that require the child to compare, add, or subtract the amounts. Are there more rubber bands or paper clips? How many more? If three thumbtacks are taken away, how many are left?

6. Help the student practice using ordinal numbers by lining up objects such as books, pencils, and trading cards and giving them an ordinal number. (Book 1 is the first, book 2 is the second.) Ask the child to identify the first, the second, and so on. Pose questions that encourage the child to use ordinal numbers. Where is the purple pencil? Allow the child to pose questions to you as you model how to use the vocabulary.

7. Locate the children's book *Alexander, Who Used to Be Rich Last Sunday* by Judith Viorst (Atheneum, 1985). After reading the story with the student, help him or her add up all the items Alexander bought. What is the total amount of money Alexander spent? Pose questions to the child about what he or she would buy if he or she suddenly became rich. Have the student estimate the cost of the items and then add up the total.

> **Helpful Hint:** Remind the child of the importance of including dollar signs and decimal points in money problems.

8. Make a place value chart by turning a paper horizontally, dividing it in thirds, and writing the labels *ones, tens,* and *hundreds* at the top of the sections. Write the digits 0–9 on blank index cards. Make more than one set so that the child can practice naming the same digit in more than one column. Select three cards, place them on the place value chart, and ask the child to read the number. On scratch paper, have the child practice writing the number in expanded form to help him or her

> **Helpful Hint:** Remind the child that a comma is used between the thousands and hundreds place so that larger numbers may be read more easily.

understand the value of the number read. (873 = 800 + 70 + 3.) As the child becomes proficient with three places, add a column for thousands and then for ten thousands. The same skill may be practiced by using dice, a deck of cards, or a numbered spinner.

9. Cut out items and their prices from a catalog and glue them on index cards. Have the student add and subtract money amounts. How much would three items cost? How much change should you get from a twenty dollar bill? This skill can be reinforced by playing a value game with letters or words. Create a chart listing the letters of the alphabet from A to Z. Assign a value to each letter: A = $.01, B = $.02, and so on. How much is your name worth? Have the student determine the values of other names and compare the values. Encourage him or her to think aloud while working. Why do different names have different values?

hundreds	tens	ones
8	7	3

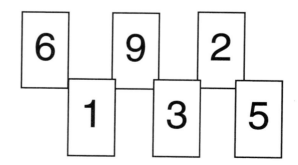

 Name

Number Knowledge

①

②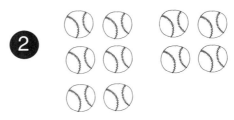

_____ + _____ = _____   _____ − _____ = _____

Use the number line to solve the problems. Count forward to add. Count back to subtract.

0 1 2 3 4 5 6 7 8 9 10 11 12

③ $6 + 4 =$ _____ $7 + 5 =$ _____

  $9 - 5 =$ _____ $8 - 8 =$ _____

④ 3,526   What number is in the hundreds place? _____

⑤ 691   What number is in the tens place? _____

Subtract.   Add.

⑥   10   ⑦   84   ⑧   9   ⑨   31
     -9 -23 $+8$ $+45$

⑩ Put the numbers in order from least to greatest. 129, 161, 101, 131

[   ]   [   ]   [   ]   [   ]

FS122130 The Tutor's Handbook: Math Grade 2

 **On the Road**

Solve each problem. Watch the signs!

1   = _____

2   −   = _____

3   22
    + 11

4   81
    + 62

5   99
    − 90

6   55
    − 21

Circle the larger number.

7   908   809

8   232   322

9 Put these numbers in order from least to greatest.

15, 13, 10, 18, 21 ☐ ☐ ☐ ☐ ☐

10 Put these numbers in order from greatest to least.

53, 47, 44, 35, 29 ☐ ☐ ☐ ☐ ☐

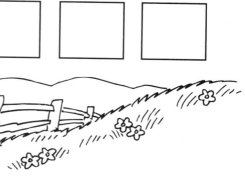

FS122130 The Tutor's Handbook: Math Grade 2

Name

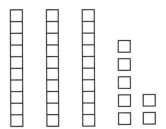 **Gone Fishing**

How many hundreds, tens, and ones? Write the number on the line.

1 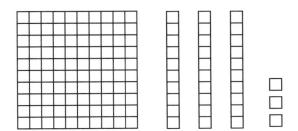 _____

2 _____

3 _____

Use the number line to add and subtract.

0 1 2 3 4 5 6 7 8 9 10 11 12

4 5 + 6 = _____   **5** 4 + 8 = _____

6 10 − 9 = _____   **7** 12 − 6 = _____

8 11 − 2 = _____   **9** 7 + 5 = _____

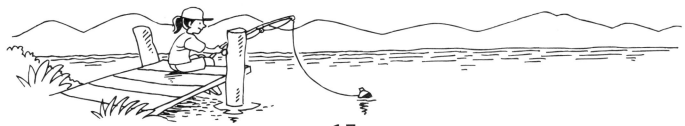

17
reproducible

Name

A Number of Colors

Subtract. Use counting beans or cubes if needed.

1
```
   8
 - 5
```

2
```
  55
- 33
```

3
```
  12
- 12
```

4
```
  44
- 33
```

5
```
  $1.25
-  1.03
```

6
```
  $2.74
-  2.01
```

7
```
  $2.99
-  2.50
```

8 A farmer picks 12 bushels of apples. He sells 3 bushels at the market. How many bushels does he have left?

9 Color $\frac{1}{2}$ of the circle blue.

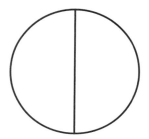

10 Color $\frac{1}{4}$ of the circle green.

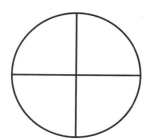

FS122130 The Tutor's Handbook: Math Grade 2

 **Name**

  ## Slam Dunk!

Use the number line to solve the problems below. Count forward to add. Count backward to subtract.

0 1 2 3 4 5 6 7 8 9 10 11 12

1
```
   10
 +  2
```

2
```
   8
 − 6
```

3
```
   3
 + 4
```

4
```
   11
 +  1
```

5 How much of the circle is shaded? _____

Add or subtract the money amounts.

6
```
  $1.09
 + 1.40
```

7
```
  $1.99
 − 1.33
```

Subtract.

8
```
   76
 − 14
```

Add.

9
```
   23
 + 56
```

PATTERNS

CONCEPTS SECOND GRADERS SHOULD KNOW

- identifying, creating, and extending geometric and number patterns
- the 1–100 number chart
- skip counting by twos, fives, and tens
- fact families

Activities

Helpful Hint:
Finding patterns and using them to solve problems helps students develop the thinking skills that lead to success with algebra.

1. Cut poster board into 1" x 10" strips. Ask the child to create a pattern by gluing dried beans onto the strips. Wooden craft sticks, tongue depressors, or twigs would work well also. Vary the activity by having the student use markers or paints to color the strips and beans.

2. Search for a quilt that contains a repeating pattern. If you can't find one around the house, look through old craft or sewing magazines. Ask the child to find the pattern sewn into the fabric. Extend this activity by asking the child to create his or her own quilt square. Bring small pieces of fabric and allow the child to select, cut out, and arrange the pieces into a quilt pattern. If possible, help the child sew the pieces together by hand. This activity can be modified by using graph paper or colored cardstock and yarn.

3. Use coins to create and reinforce patterns. Help the student arrange 100 pennies into groups of 10 on a large piece of paper and then write the correct number next to each group. Ask the child to practice different arrangements—vertical, horizontal, or various number groupings. Vary this activity by using different coins to create the pattern. Remind the child to think out loud while working to explain why he or she chose the patterns.

4. Fact families are addition and subtraction or multiplication and division facts that use the same numbers. There are four facts in each fact family. Write out a math problem that the child knows, such as $7 + 8 = 15$. Help the child see that he or she also knows that $8 + 7 = 15$, $15 - 8 = 7$ and $15 - 7 = 8$. Give the child the numbers for a fact family and ask him or her to write all of the facts. Practice with this helps the child memorize basic math facts.

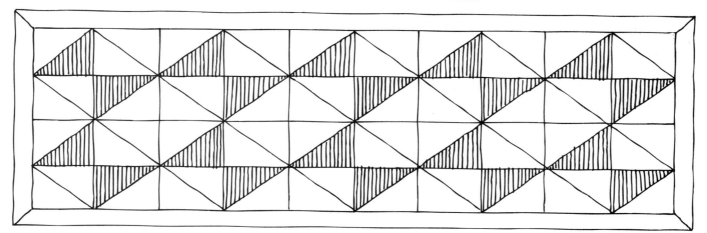

5. Find various real-life objects for the student to arrange into patterns. If you live near a beach, go searching for sea shells. Hunt through the meadows to find wildflowers. Walk through the woods to find tree branches or leaves. Stroll down the street to find discarded items. Have the child bring in his or her favorite trading cards. Locate books of various sizes in the library. Look through old magazines for pictures. Have the student arrange the items into a pattern. Ask him or her to explain why he or she arranged the items that way.

6. Give the child a 1–100 number chart (page 22) that has been cut into strips of tens. Help the child to put the chart back in the correct order without looking at a finished chart.

Helpful Hint: Counting objects by numbers other than one can be accomplished much more quickly than counting one object at a time. Finding and using counting patterns will make solving difficult problems easier.

7. Help the child identify a sequence pattern on the 1–100 number chart (24, 27, ___, 33, 36, ___). Have him or her cover each number given in the sequence with a counting bean. Encourage the child to look for a pattern to help name the missing numbers. Practice both forward and backward number sequences to help the child develop this skill. Remind him or her that it is important to look at the entire list of numbers before looking for the answer. Give the child a list of numbers in a sequence. Would 35 be in this sequence? Why or why not?

8. Skip counting means skipping numbers as you count by groups other than one. For the student to skip count by three, have him or her place a counter on the number three, skip two squares and place another counter on the third number. The student should continue covering numbers for three rows. Ask the child to name the numbers and describe the pattern. Repeat the process with other numbers. As children become more comfortable, vary the difficulty of the problems you present. Start at 36. Skip count by 3 and end at 52. Which numbers will you cover? Name the odd numbers between 63 and 87. Ask the child to practice skip counting as he or she jumps rope, saying one number with each jump.

Helpful Hint: Using counters (dried beans or popcorn seeds) to cover the numbers on the number chart enables the child to look for patterns and use the chart again and again.

1—100 Number Chart

1	2	3	4	5	6	7	8	9	10
11	12	13	14	15	16	17	18	19	20
21	22	23	24	25	26	27	28	29	30
31	32	33	34	35	36	37	38	39	40
41	42	43	44	45	46	47	48	49	50
51	52	53	54	55	56	57	58	59	60
61	62	63	64	65	66	67	68	69	70
71	72	73	74	75	76	77	78	79	80
81	82	83	84	85	86	87	88	89	90
91	92	93	94	95	96	97	98	99	100

FS122130 The Tutor's Handbook: Math Grade 2

Create a Pattern

1 **Choose three different colors.**
Design a color pattern on the grid below.

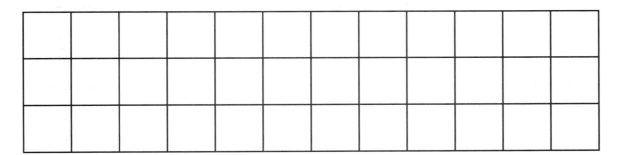

2 **Make a number pattern, using these numbers: 0, 1, 2, 3**

3 **Complete the patterns.**

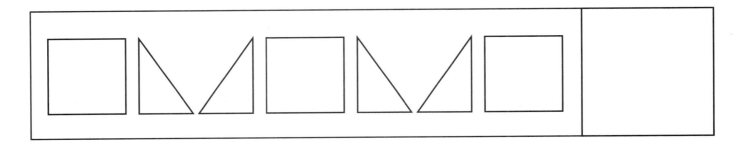

FS122130 The Tutor's Handbook: Math Grade 2

 Name

Perfect Patterns

Cut out the shapes. Draw around the shapes to make patterns on another piece of paper.

24
reproducible

FS122130 The Tutor's Handbook: Math Grade 2

Number Patterns

Skip count by two. Color those numbers blue. Skip count by five. Colors those numbers green.

1	2	3	4	5	6	7	8	9	10
11	12	13	14	15	16	17	18	19	20
21	22	23	24	25	26	27	28	29	30
31	32	33	34	35	36	37	38	39	40
41	42	43	44	45	46	47	48	49	50
51	52	53	54	55	56	57	58	59	60
61	62	63	64	65	66	67	68	69	70
71	72	73	74	75	76	77	78	79	80
81	82	83	84	85	86	87	88	89	90
91	92	93	94	95	96	97	98	99	100

1 When skip counting by two, will you color the number 18? _____

43? _____   79? _____   100? _____

2 When skip counting by five, will you color the number 25? _____

61? _____   80? _____   100? _____

 Name

   # Pattern Problems

Complete the patterns.

 1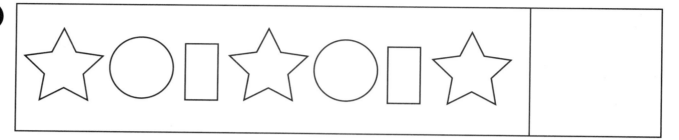

2

3 Write two addition and two subtraction facts for fact family.

      3 2 5   4 8 12

_____   _____

_____   _____

_____   _____

_____   _____

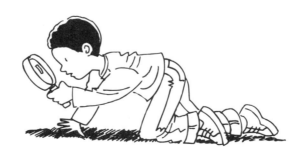

FS122130 The Tutor's Handbook: Math Grade 2

 **Name**

The Pattern Expert

Put an X on the number that does not belong in each pattern.

1   3   6   8   9   12   15

2   2   4   6   7   8   10

Write *yes* or *no*.

3   If you were skip counting by two, would you count 16? _____

     39? _____   76? _____

4   **Complete the pattern.**

Fill in the missing numbers.

5   5, _____, 15, 20, _____, 30, _____, 40, 45, _____

6   20, 30, _____, 50, 60, _____, 80, _____, 100

27
reproducible

FS122130 The Tutor's Handbook: Math Grade 2

CONCEPTS SECOND GRADERS SHOULD KNOW

- identifying and describing two- and three-dimensional figures
- classifying shapes by the number and shape of faces, edges, and vertices
- congruent shapes
- the relationship of various shapes (for example, there are two triangles in a square)

Activities

Helpful Hint: It is important for the student to learn and use correct geometric vocabulary. Model and encourage correct usage when manipulating objects or problem solving.

1. Go on a Geometry Hunt around the building, playground, or in the neighborhood. Help the child search for geometric structures and shapes. Look for buildings in the shapes of cubes or for rectangular windows and doors. Find the cylindrical shape of a telephone pole. Explain that some shapes may be hidden and encourage the child to practice looking with a "geometric eye." Have the child record the shapes and locations in his or her math journal.

2. Bring in cardboard tubes (paper towel or bathroom tissue rolls), straws, cone-shaped party hats, various boxes, and other three-dimensional geometric figures for the student to use to design a playground. Remind him or her that some playgrounds have tire swings, barrels to crawl through, boxes for climbing, and see-saws (a long, rectangular plank). Have the child take you on a tour of the playground, naming each shape and its function. Encourage creativity and imagination!

3. Encourage the child to create an artistic masterpiece with colored paper! Provide lots of pieces of construction paper that have been cut into various geometric shapes such as triangles, squares, rectangles, and circles. Ask the child to arrange the shapes in a design. If the child has trouble getting started, you might suggest a train, a barn, a Ferris wheel, or an animal. Encourage the child to use his or her imagination when designing. While he or she is gluing the shapes onto a large piece of plain paper, ask the child to identify the shapes and explain how they work together. Why did you use these shapes to design an elephant? What about the triangle reminded you of a fish?

4. Serve ice cream cones! Top each cone with a sphere of ice cream. Discuss the shapes. Ask the child why a cone is shaped that way. Encourage creative thinking. Ask the student to imagine different shapes to hold ice cream. Which is the best shape? Why?

5. Play the game "I See A . . ." by identifying shapes such as circles, cones, triangles, rectangles, rectangular prisms, squares, spheres, cylinders, and cubes. The first player calls out a geometric shape he or she sees in the immediate area. For example, "I see a rectangle." The second player guesses which object is being referred to. "Is it the table?" If two or more children are being tutored, have each child take turns playing the game. This game is fun and easy to play both indoors and out!

6. Have the child make a shape collage by cutting out pictures from magazines. He or she might use a cereal box, a can of vegetables, a baseball, an Egyptian pyramid, a party hat, a building block, or a paper cup. Paste these on a large sheet of paper. Ask the child to identify each shape.

7. Discuss elements of geometric shapes. Search for ways to help the child remember and identify the shapes. Provide real models as you explain the difference between space and plane figures. For example, a square has a flat surface, while a cube has eight sides. A cone has no edges or corners, while a pyramid has both. A circle has a flat surface, while a sphere is spherical (like a globe).

8. Two figures are congruent if they are exactly the same size and shape. They can be placed on top of each other to verify that they match exactly. Remind the child that it may help to turn a shape to see if it is congruent with another shape.

9. Ask the child why a cone, cylinder, and sphere can roll smoothly, but a rectangular prism, cube, or pyramid can not. (They have corners.) Demonstrate these principles with an ice cream cone, a ball, and dice. Encourage the child to explain his or her thinking process while deciding the answer.

Helpful Hint: Use geoboards (available at your local teacher supply store) and rubber bands when demonstrating geometric shapes.

10. Origami is a terrific tool for learning about shape relationships. Check the local library for books about origami such as *Easy Origami* by Gary M. Gross and Tina Weintraub (Scholastic, 1996). While you teach the child how to construct a simple figure, reinforce the names of shapes and how they relate to each other. For example, take a rectangle and fold it into two squares.

11. Prepare the student for learning about perimeter by using rulers or yardsticks to help the child measure the sides of objects in the room (for example, a rectangular mirror, a window, a door, a small rug). The child can record the measurements in a journal by drawing and labeling the objects they have measured. Explain that to find the perimeter, measure the outside of an object and add up the all of the sides.

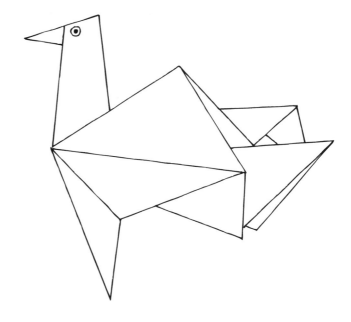

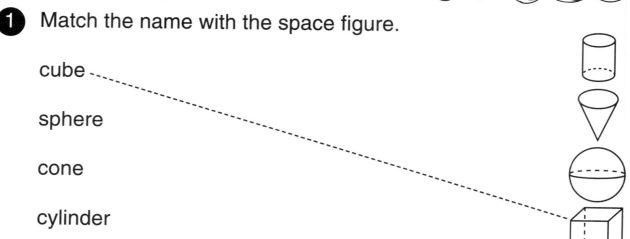

Smooth Sailing

1 Match the name with the space figure.

cube

sphere

cone

cylinder

2 Draw the following plane figures:

square	rectangle	triangle

3 Show how you can divide a square into 2 triangles.

FS122130 The Tutor's Handbook: Math Grade 2

 Name

 # Secret Shapes

Find the plane figures in the picture.
Count the number. Fill in the chart. Color the picture.

_____ triangles   _____ squares

_____ circles   _____ rectangles

Extra Practice: On another piece of paper, create your own picture with a cube, rectangular prism, cone, pyramid, cylinder, and sphere.

FS122130 The Tutor's Handbook: Math Grade 2

 Name   # The Shapeshifter

Cut out the shapes. Trace them on another piece of paper to make as many as you want. Use them to make new shapes. What new shapes did you make?

 **Name**

Super Shapes

Some shapes have edges, corners, and sides.
Count how many.

1 How many sides? _____

How many edges? _____

How many corners? _____

2 How many sides? _____

How many edges? _____

How many corners? _____

3 Are the shapes congruent? Write *yes* or *no*.

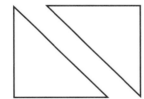

_____   _____

4 Draw a line of symmetry through each figure.

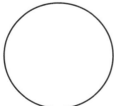

Name

Geometry Genius

1 Circle the plane figures.

triangle	cube	circle	pyramid	square

2 Circle the space figures.

rectangle	cone	oval	sphere	cylinder

3 Combine two triangles to form a square.

4 Are the shapes congruent? Write *yes* or *no*.

_____   _____

34
reproducible

FS122130 The Tutor's Handbook: Math Grade 2

CONCEPTS SECOND GRADERS SHOULD KNOW

- standard and nonstandard units of measurement
- estimating measurements
- length to the nearest inch or centimeter
- time to the nearest five minutes
- number of minutes in an hour, days in a month, weeks in a year
- elapsed time in hours
- U.S. customary and metric measurements for mass/weight, temperature, length, volume, and capacity
- using a calendar

Activities

1. Explain that the human foot was once used as a unit of measure in England, but is now

Scale: I 👣 = I foot

considered a non-standard unit of measurement there. In a heel-to-toe movement, walk the length of the room. How many "feet" did it take to walk the room? Why would it be a different number for a child than for an adult? Help the child measure the room with a yardstick. Was the estimate correct? Have the student draw a diagram of the room and label the measurements. Make it fun and encourage the student to draw a key with a small foot to show scale.

Helpful Hint: Begin measurement with nonstandard units of measure such as paper clips. Once the child has mastered that, move on to standard units of measure.

2. Cut a piece of string or ribbon exactly 12 inches long. Give it to the child to measure any items or objects that are immediately available. What objects are exactly 12 inches? Is your forearm more or less than the ribbon? Is the table top more or less than the string? Is your pencil less than the ribbon? Have the student record objects in his or her journal with words or pictures.

3. Provide a calendar. A large, twelve-month wall calendar works well. Explain to the student how the year is divided into 12 months, 52 weeks, 365 days, and 4 seasons. Draw outlines around each season or fill in the days with a seasonal symbol (orange leaves for fall, snowflakes for winter). Discuss elapsed time. Ask the child to count the number of days until the weekend. Let the child record events such as birthdays, holidays, or other expected activities. How long has it been since winter break? Since summer break? How many more weeks until your birthday?

4. Practice telling time with digital and analog clocks. Ask the student questions about elapsed time. If you started your homework at 2:00 and finished at 2:30, how long did it take you to do your homework? Keep the questions simple. A teaching clock (one with moveable hands) allows the child to manipulate the hands for better practice.

Helpful Hint: Time is an abstract concept that takes time to master. Be patient with the student while he or she is learning to tell time.

5. Provide water, sand, rice, or cornmeal for measuring. Allow plenty of time for the student to practice filling cup, pint, quart, gallon, and liter containers. If possible, provide a balance scale to compare weights. If not, comparisons can be made with familiar objects (for example, a gallon of milk is heavier than a pint). How many cups does it take to fill a quart? A gallon? How many liters are in a large plastic soda bottle? How many cups is that? Which is heavier, the dictionary or the coloring book? Is the brick heavier than the shoebox?

6. Place a thermometer (Fahrenheit and/or Celsius) outside and have the child record the readings for a week. Use an almanac to help the child find the average minimum and maximum temperature for two months in two different cities, including his or her own. How does this information compare with the student's findings? Ask the child to illustrate the appropriate clothes to wear in each city for the two months. Given the temperatures, what outdoor activities would be appropriate? Ask the student to record ideas or drawings in his or her math journal.

7. Prepare a simple recipe, such as instant pudding (make sure to get a parent's permission). Have the child read the directions on the package (help with reading as necessary). Measure the amount of dried pudding mix. How many cups? Help the child pour the milk as called for by the directions. Prepare the pudding as directed. Enjoy the tasty treat!

Metric	U.S. Customary
length 1 centimeter = 10 millimeters 1 decimeter = 10 centimeters 1 meter = 10 decimeters **mass/weight** 1 kilogram = 1,000 grams **capacity** 1 liter = 1,000 milliliters	**length** 1 foot = 12 inches 1 yard = 3 feet 1 mile = 5,280 feet **mass/weight** 1 pound = 16 ounces 1 ton = 2,000 pounds **capacity** 1 cup = 8 fluid ounces 1 pint = 2 cups 1 quart = 2 pints 1 gallon = 4 quarts

8. Ask the child to question five people whom he or she knows well (family members would be ideal) about their heights and weights. Have the student record each person's name, height, and weight in his or her math journal. At the next tutoring session, help the child record the heights and weights onto a chart or illustrated diagram. Who is the tallest (highest)? Who is the shortest (lowest)? Who is the heaviest? The lightest?

Helpful Hint: Some second graders are inexperienced with standard measurements. Some students may need assistance learning how to read an inch or centimeter ruler.

9. Select one of the child's personal interests or hobbies—camping, trading cards, crafts, roller skating—and explore ways of using measurement while enjoying this activity. How long does it take to skate 100 yards? What is the length of a trading card? How many centimeters of yarn will be needed for this craft project?

10. Drop a few small rocks into three plastic containers and place one narcissus bulb (avail- able at home and garden centers) on top of the rocks in each container. Help the student to add enough water to reach just below—not touching—the bottoms of the bulbs. (The water level should be kept constant throughout the blooming period.) Each tutoring session ask the student to observe, measure, and record results in his or her math journal. Make a chart or mark a calendar that tells the day of the month the bulb was placed in water and the date the first sprouts appeared. Measure the sprouts each session. When blooms appear, compare the different heights of the plants. Which plant is the tallest? Which plant has the most blooms? Measurements should be made in both inches and centimeters.

 Name

1 2 3 4 5 6 # Measure Up 7 8 9 10 11 12

1 Use paper clips as units for measuring.

	Estimate	Measure
a. pencil	_____ paper clips	_____ paper clips
b. notepad	_____ paper clips	_____ paper clips

2 Use a ruler to measure the string.

The string is _____ inches long.

3 Draw a line 4 inches long.

4 Circle the one that weighs more. **5** Circle the one that weighs less.

38
reproducible

 Name

How Long Is It?

Use a ruler to measure each string.

1 —————————————————— ____ inches

2 ——————— ____ centimeters

3 ————————— ____ inches

Draw a line that measures

4 6 inches

5 3 inches

6 7 centimeters

7 15 centimeters

8 Draw a picture of an object that you estimate to be about 10 feet long.

Measurement

Mammoth Measurements

Look at the pictures.

Circle the one that weighs more.

 1

2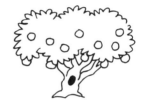

3

4

Circle the one that holds more.

5

6

Circle the one that is hotter.

7

8

Which measurement would you use? Circle one.

9 to measure milk   inches   liters   centimeters

10 to weigh a dog   pounds   inches   meters

FS122130 The Tutor's Handbook: Math Grade 2

 **Time for Money**

Count the money.

1   _____

2  _____

3 Write > or <.

87¢   68¢

_____

Use coins to help solve this problem.

4 An apple costs $0.46. You have $0.50. If you bought the apple, how

much money would you have left? _____

Write in the correct times.

5 _____   **6** _____   **7** _____   **8** _____

9 If Jose has a birthday on Monday, and Nellie's birthday is four days

later, on what day is Nellie's birthday? _____

FS122130 The Tutor's Handbook: Math Grade 2

 **Name**

Measurement Madness

1 Use a ruler to measure the yarn.

a. _____ _____ inches

b. _____ _____ centimeters

2 Circle the one that weighs more. Put an X on the one that weighs less.

3 Fill in the hands on the clock to tell the time.

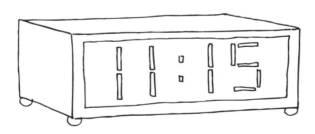

4 If you had $1.33 and you bought a book that cost $1.09, how much

change would you get back? _____

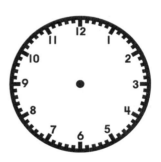

FS122130 The Tutor's Handbook: Math Grade 2

CONCEPTS SECOND GRADERS SHOULD KNOW

- collecting, organizing, and displaying data
- using tables, graphs, and charts to evaluate data
- asking and answering simple questions about a graph
- the likelihood of an event

Activities

1. Help the child to take a survey of his or her clothes closet as a way of recording data. Help the student create a table showing the number of shoes, shirts, pants, coats, and hats making a tally mark for each item. Show the child how to make a crosshatch on every fifth tally mark. Help the child make a bar graph using the data on the tally sheet. Which clothes item do you have the most of? The least?

2. Help the student take a survey of food items found in a kitchen cabinet or refrigerator such as milk products, pasta, soup, fresh vegetables and fruits, and cereals. Tally the results and write the totals. What food items make up the greatest number? The lowest number?

3. Teach probability by placing 6 black tokens and 3 yellow tokens (checkers, crayons, or small squares of paper work well, too) in a small paper bag. Ask the child to predict what color will be drawn. Draw one token at a time. Repeat 12 times. Remember to return the token after each draw. Record how many times the prediction was correct. Encourage the child to explain his or her reasoning for the prediction.

Helpful Hint: Probability is the prediction or analysis of the likelihood that a certain event will occur. Something is equally likely to happen if all of the possible outcomes have the same chance of occurring.

4. Another way to reinforce probability concepts is to use a spinner. Using a marker, divide a paper plate or cardboard circle into fourths. Color three-fourths of the plate purple. Color one-fourth of the plate green. As you are coloring the circle, introduce fractions by explaining and naming the fraction you are creating. In the center attach a pointer made from posterboard or cardstock. Use a brad to fasten the pointer. Ask the child to predict how many times you will land on the purple or the green and record the results. Spin the hand 12 times. How many times did the spinner land on purple? On green? Were the child's predictions correct? Before you spin, encourage the child to predict which color will be spun more often. Pose questions that require the child to provide reasoning for the prediction. Extend this activity by tallying the results of 20 spins. Help the child create a bar graph displaying the results. Ask the child to interpret the graph and record the data in his or her journal. How many more times did the spinner land on purple? The activity may also be varied by making different proportions on the plate. Try one-fourth green, one-fourth blue, and one-half purple. Pose similar questions about probability.

Helpful Hint: Vary the orientation of graphs. Present some graphs vertically and some horizontally.

5. Show the student a pictograph of trading cards. Help the child learn how to read the pictograph. Show him or her the key and explain that the symbol usually represents a specified number of items. In the example below, one card equals ten trading cards. Then show the child how to count the symbols on the graph. Pose simple questions about the graph. Who has the most trading cards? How many does she have? Encourage the child to create his or her own pictograph.

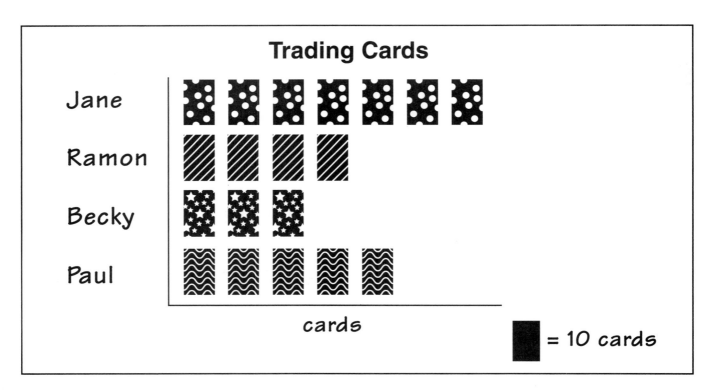

Trading Cards

Jane
Ramon
Becky
Paul

cards

■ = 10 cards

   Cars For Sale

1 A used car lot has 5 blue cars, 8 black cars, 4 white cars, and 2 red cars for sale. Complete the bar graph, showing each color.

Cars For Sale

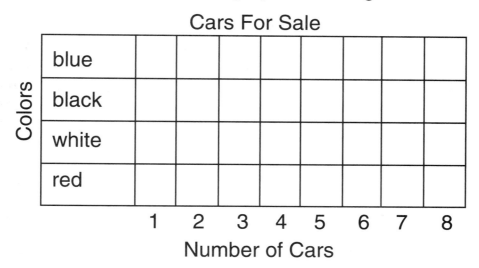

How many cars are for sale? _____

The used car lot has the most cars in what color?_____

2 If you spin the color wheel 10 times, which color do you think it will

land on the most? _____

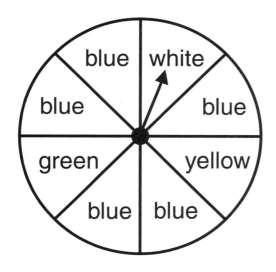

FS122130 The Tutor's Handbook: Math Grade 2

 Name

 # Take a Survey

Survey your friends and family about the activities they enjoyed this week. Make a tally mark for each answer. Record the total.

Weekly Activities		
Activity	Tally	Total
Movie		
Sports event		
Shopping		
Playing games		
Using a computer		
Skate boarding		
Watching TV		

1 Which activity had the greatest number?_____

2 Which activity had the lowest number?_____

3 Which activities had the same number? _____

Make a bar graph or pictograph of the survey results on the back of this paper.

FS122130 The Tutor's Handbook: Math Grade 2

 Name

Wacky Weather

Weather for One Week

		snow	
		rain	
		sun	

| | Mon. | Tues. | Wed. | Thurs. | Fri. | Sat. | Sun. |

1 How many days of were there? _____

2 How many days of were there? _____

Using the bar graph, answer the questions below.

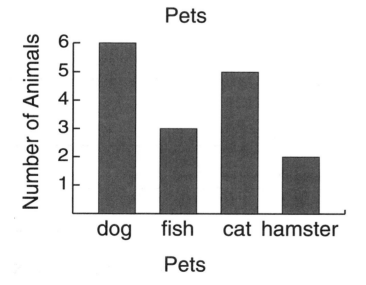

Pets

Number of Animals

dog   fish   cat hamster

Pets

3 How many people have cats? _____ Dogs? _____

4 Which pet is the most popular? _____

 Name _____

 Make a Prediction

Look at the spinners.
Which number do you think the spinner will land on more often?
Circle the number.

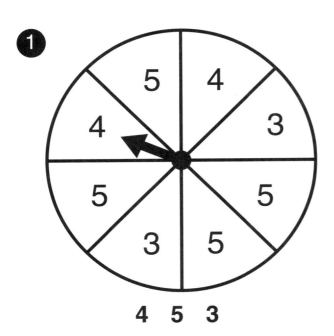

4   5   3

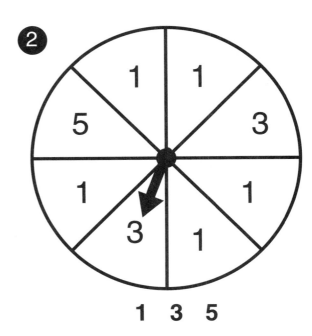

1   3   5

Which color do you think the spinner will land on more often?

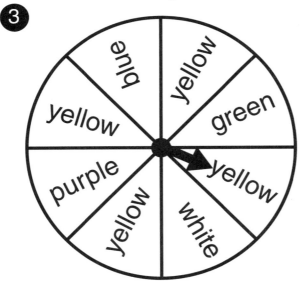

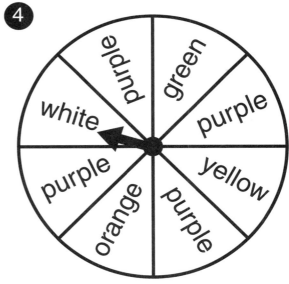

_____   _____

 Name

  Favorite Foods

1 Look at the tally chart. Make a bar graph, filling in one block for each time the food was eaten.

Favorite Food

Food	Tally
Hamburger	卌 I
Hot Dog	IIII
Pizza	卌 IIII

Favorite Food

Hamburger									
Hot Dog									
Pizza									

Which food is the favorite? _____

Which food is the least favorite? _____

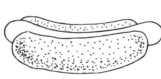 

2 John asked all of his classmates what their favorite colors were. Ten people said blue. Six people said orange. Four people said purple. Tally the results of John's survey. Show the results on a bar graph. Color the bar graph.

Color	Tally
blue	
orange	
purple	

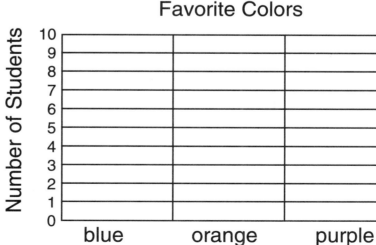

Favorite Colors

Number of Students

10, 9, 8, 7, 6, 5, 4, 3, 2, 1, 0

blue   orange   purple

Colors

FS122130 The Tutor's Handbook: Math Grade 2

PROBLEM SOLVING

It is important to help the child to understand that he or she is developing a variety of strategies that will help him or her solve math problems. A strategy is simply a plan that may be used to solve a problem. Choosing an appropriate strategy is the challenge. A sufficient understanding of the different strategies the child has mastered will enable him or her to think the problem through and select the best one to use to solve a particular problem.

> **Helpful Hint:** Be sensitive to the child's reading level. Let the child do the math, but help him or her with the reading.

If the child is unsuccessful in solving a problem, help him or her with an alternative approach to the problem. Talking through a number of different problems helps the child develop more sophisticated problem solving skills. In fact, the process that the student goes through to solve the problem is as important as the correct solution.

As you help the student solve a variety of problems, encourage him or her to recall some of the strategies he or she has developed.

Can you make a table or graph with the information?

Would it help you to draw a picture?

Can you combine some of the numbers to make them easier to work with?

What is the problem asking?

Which operation should you use?

What are the key words in the problem that help you know what to do?

Does the problem require more than one step? Which step is first?

Is there information missing that is needed to solve the problem?

Does the problem contain unnecessary information?

Can you find a pattern?

Can you make a guess and test the answer?

As you work with the child, remember the benefit of having him or her talk about his or her thinking process. Respond and ask additional questions that will help the child discover that there is often more than one way to solve a given problem. Help the child evaluate these possibilities and determine the best course of action.

Remind children of the steps necessary to solve a problem.

think	What is the problem asking?
search	What facts does the problem give? How will I solve it?
solve	Compute the answer—this may require more than one step.
check	Does my answer make sense? Does it answer the question?

Consider listing these steps on a chart and continually review the steps until they become automatic.

 Name

 # Solve the Problem

Solve the problems.

1 Julia had 2 pages of math homework, plus 1 page left from yesterday. Maria had 3 pages of social studies and 1 page left from yesterday. How many pages did both children have altogether?

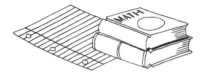

2 Cedric received $5.00 for his birthday. He wants to rent a video game that costs $3.25. How much will he have left?

3 Mario wants a notebook that costs $5.00 at Super "A" Store. His brother wants the same notebook. How much will two of these notebooks cost?

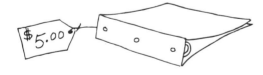

Draw a line through the information you do not need. Solve.

4 In Browntown, seven inches of rain fell in one day. It had not rained in two weeks. In Blue View, four inches of rain fell on the same day. What was the difference in rainfall between the two towns?

 **Name**

 # What's the Problem?

Circle the operation and solve each problem.

---

1 Twelve friends are invited to your birthday party. Each person brings one friend. How many people are at the party? Don't forget to count yourself.

+

−

x

÷ _____

---

2 On a visit to the zoo, you see new baby animals. The camel has 1 calf. The elephant has 1 calf. The bear has 2 cubs. The monkey has 2 babies. How many new baby animals do you see?

+

−

x

÷ _____

---

3 There are 6 cups of punch on the table. Six children are sitting at the table. If each child gets one cup, how many cups will be left?

+

−

x

÷ _____

 Name

 # Problem Detective

On each line, write the word or words that give you a clue about how to solve the problem. Then solve each problem.

1 There are 3 plates on the table. Each plate has 2 cookies. How

many cookies are there in all? _____

2 A classroom has 4 rows of chairs. Each row has 3 chairs. What is

the total number of chairs in the room? _____

3 There are 8 birds sitting on one telephone wire. If 2 birds fly away,

how many are left? _____

4 The fiction section in the library contains 290 volumes of books. The
mystery section contains 149 volumes. How many books are there

in both sections? _____

FS122130 The Tutor's Handbook: Math Grade 2

Name

 **Fishing for Problems**

Draw a line through the information you do not need. Solve each problem.

1 A fisherman caught 130 pounds of fish on Monday. The outside temperature reached 85 degrees. On Tuesday, he caught 166 pounds. How many more pounds did he catch on Tuesday than on Monday?

2 The driver in the winning race car clocked in at 189 miles per hour. Sally Speedster had a new car and 4 new tires. The driver in second place clocked in at 175 miles per hour. What was the difference in miles per hour between the first and second place cars?

3 On a family farm in Virginia there were 24 cows. At least 6 of the cows were black and white. The farm also had 12 horses and 3 goats. How many animals were on the farm?

4 How many more people live in Oakwood than Hickoryville?
   Hickoryville has a population of 247.
   Hickoryville has 4 miles of paved roads.
   Oakwood has a population of 558.

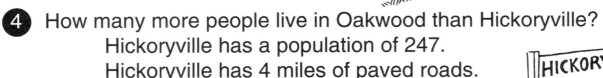

HICKORYVILLE
Pop. 247

FS122130 The Tutor's Handbook: Math Grade 2

  # Nature Walk

1 Eduardo has 12 blue marbles in his collection. James has 15 green marbles in his collection. Sue has 20 red marbles in her collection. How many marbles do the three students have altogether?

Which operation is needed to solve the problem? _____

What word or words gave you a clue? _____

Solve the problem. _____marbles

2 While taking a nature walk,
Jesse noticed the following things:
    14 types of trees
    8 types of flowers
    7 types of birds
    3 small animals

On the back of this paper, write a
story problem with the information given.
Solve the problem.

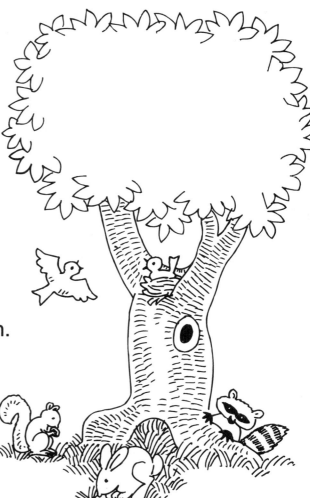

 Name

 Let's Review

Write an addition or subtraction sentence for each group.

1

2

_____ + _____ = _____   _____ – _____ = _____

Solve each problem. Watch the signs!

3
$$\begin{array}{r} 86 \\ + 11 \\ \hline \end{array}$$

4
$$\begin{array}{r} \$2.30 \\ + 1.40 \\ \hline \end{array}$$

5
$$\begin{array}{r} 65 \\ - 54 \\ \hline \end{array}$$

6
$$\begin{array}{r} \$1.82 \\ - 1.51 \\ \hline \end{array}$$

Use > or <.

7 830 ____ 560

8 293 ____ 308

9 Put these numbers in order from least to greatest.
25, 40, 35, 20, 45, 30

_____

10 How much of the circle is shaded?

_____

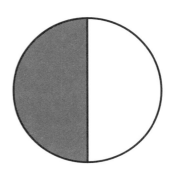

FS122130 The Tutor's Handbook: Math Grade 2

 **Name**

Let's Review

1 Make a pattern, using the colors brown and yellow.

2 Put an X on the numbers that do not belong in the pattern.

2	4	5	6	8	9	10	12	14	15	16	18	20

3 Complete the pattern.

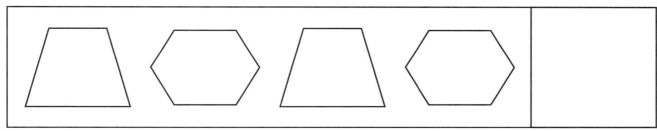

4 If you were skip counting by 2, would you count 18? Write *yes* or *no*.

_____

5 Complete the sequence.

120, 130, _____, 150, _____, 170, _____, 190, _____

6 Write the fact family for 9, 8, 17.

_____   _____

_____   _____

FS122130 The Tutor's Handbook: Math Grade 2

 **Name**

Let's Review

1 Match the words with the correct space figures.

a. cube

b. cone

c. pyramid

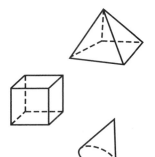

2 Circle the plane figures.

          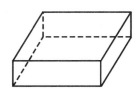   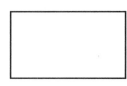

triangle   rectangular prism   cylinder   rectangle

3 Divide the circle into 8 equal parts.

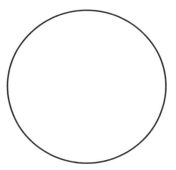

4 Draw a line of symmetry through the square.

FS122130 The Tutor's Handbook: Math Grade 2

 Name

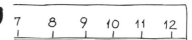

Let's Review

1 Use a ruler to measure the string.

a. _____ inches

b. _____ centimeters

2 Circle the one that weighs more.

3 Which is the best measurement to use? Circle one.

to measure a park	liters	meters	inches
to measure a trophy	meters	centimeters	cups
to measure some apple juice	cups	inches	kilometers

4 Write the correct time below each clock.

_____

_____

 Name

 # Let's Review

A fruit basket contains 8 apples, 5 bananas, 4 pears, and 6 oranges. Complete the table, showing the tally for each.

Fruit	Tally
apples	
bananas	
pears	
oranges	

1 How many pieces of fruit are in the basket? _____

2 How many apples are in the basket? _____

3 How many more bananas than pears are in the basket? _____

4 Which number do you think the spinner will land on

most often? _____

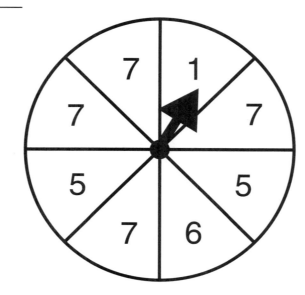

FS122130 The Tutor's Handbook: Math Grade 2

 Name

 # Let's Review

Read each problem carefully. Solve.

1 Kevin mowed the grass and was paid $10.00. If he gets paid the same amount for mowing it again next week, how much money will he have made?

_____

2 Marla unloaded 16 boxes of soft drinks before the grocery store opened. Two of the boxes were a new flavor. Later, she unloaded 7 boxes of cookies. How many boxes did she unload?

_____

3 If one classroom can seat 25 students, how many can be seated in 3 classrooms of the same size?

_____

4 Charles has 35 trading cards. He buys 5 more on Saturday. Minh has 30 trading cards. He buys 10 more on Saturday. How many cards does each boy have?

Charles _____ cards

Minh _____ cards

 # Student Survey

Read each statement. Complete the statement or circle the answer.

1 How do you feel about math now?

_____

_____

_____

_____

_____

2 How good are you at math?

not very good   ok   very good

3 I use math everyday.

true   not true

4 Which of these do you know how to do better after tutoring?

___addition   ___recognizing shapes

___subtraction   ___measuring

___reading graphs and charts   ___problem solving

5 The part of math I like best is

_____

_____

_____

6 I want to improve my math grades this year.

yes   no

62
reproducible

FS122130 The Tutor's Handbook: Math Grade 2

Answers

Page 15
1. 3 + 4 = 7
2. 6 − 4 = 2
3. 10, 12, 4, 0
4. 5
5. 9
6. 1
7. 61
8. 17
9. 76
10. 101, 129, 131, 161

Page 16
1. 8
2. 1
3. 33
4. 143
5. 9
6. 34
7. 908
8. 322
9. 10, 13, 15, 18, 21
10. 53, 47, 44, 35, 29

Page 17
1. 37
2. 133
3. 268
4. 11
5. 12
6. 1
7. 6
8. 9
9. 12

Page 18
1. 3
2. 22
3. 0
4. 11
5. $0.22
6. $0.73
7. $0.49
8. 9 bushels
9. answers will vary
10. answers will vary

Page 19
1. 12
2. 2
3. 7
4. 12
5. ¼
6. $2.49
7. $0.66
8. 62
9. 79

Page 23
1. answers will vary
2. answers will vary
3. circle, right triangle

Page 24
Answers will vary

Page 25
1. yes, no, no, yes
2. yes, no, yes, yes

Page 26
1. star
2. right triangle
6. 3 + 2 = 5, 2 + 3 = 5
   5 − 3 = 2, 5 − 2 = 3
   4 + 8 = 12, 8 + 4 = 12
   12 − 8 = 4, 12 − 4 = 8

Page 27
1. 8
2. 7
3. yes, no, yes
4. nickel
5. 10, 25, 35, 50
6. 40, 70, 90

Page 30
1.

2.

3. answers will vary

Page 31
18 triangles
10 circles
29 squares
17 rectangles

NOTE: Only major, obvious shapes counted. Number may vary depending on perspective

Page 32
Answers will vary.

Page 33
1. 6 sides, 12 edges, 8 corners
2. 5 sides, 8 edges, 5 corners
3. yes, no
4. answers will vary

Page 34
1. plane figures: triangle, circle, square
2. space figures: cone, sphere, cylinder
3. answers will vary
4. yes, no

Page 38
1. answers will vary
2. 6 inches
3. a four-inch line
4. elephant
5. flower

Page 39
1. 3 in.
2. 4 cm
3. 2 in.
4. 6 in. line
5. 3 in. line
6. 7 cm line
7. 15 cm line
8. answers will vary

Page 40
1. jug
2. truck
3. pie
4. tree
5. pitcher
6. tub
7. mug
8. campfire
9. liters
10. pounds

Page 41
1. $0.63
2. $1.43
3. >
4. $0.04
5. 6:00
6. 6:15
7. 4:45
8. 7:25
9. Friday

Answers

Page 42
1. a. 4 inches, b. 10 cm
2. circle elephant, cross out book
3. show clock hands at 11:15
4. $0.24

Page 45
1.

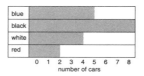

19 cars for sale,
black
2. blue

Page 46
All answers will vary.

Page 47
1. 1
2. 4
3. 5, 6
4. dogs

Page 48
1. 5
2. 1
3. yellow
4. purple

Page 49
1.

Favorite Food

Hamburger										
Hot Dog										
Pizza										

pizza, hot dog

2.

Color	Tally
blue	‖‖‖ ‖‖‖
orange	‖‖‖	
purple	‖‖‖‖

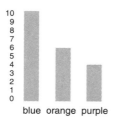

Page 51
1. 7 pages
2. $1.75
3. $10.00
4. It had not rained in two weeks.,
   3 inches

Page 52
1. addition, 25 people
2. addition, 6 babies
3. subtraction, 0 cups

Page 53
1. in all, 6 cookies
2. total number, 12 chairs
3. are left, 6 birds
4. both sections, 439

Page 54
1. The outside temperature reached
   85 degrees; 36 pounds
2. Sally Speedster had a new car
   and 4 new tires; 14 miles per hour
3. At least 6 of the cows were black
   and white. 39 animals
4. Hickoryville has 4 miles of paved
   roads. 311 people

Page 55
1. addition, altogether, 47
2. answers will vary

Page 56
1. 7 + 11 = 18
2. 5 − 5 = 0
3. 97
4. $3.70
5. 11
6. $0.31
7. >
8. <
9. 20, 25, 30, 35, 40, 45
10. ½

Page 57
1. answers will vary
2. 5, 9, 15
3.

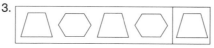

4. yes
5. 140, 160, 180, 200
6. 8 + 9 = 17, 9 + 8 = 17
   17 − 8 = 9, 17 − 9 = 8

Page 58
1.

2. triangle, rectangle
3.

4. answers will vary

Page 59
1. a. 5 in., b. 11 cm
2. circle ocean liner
3. meters
   centimeters
   cups
4. 8:15, 2:30

Page 60
1.

apples	‖‖‖ ‖‖‖
bananas	‖‖‖
pears	‖‖‖‖
oranges	‖‖‖	

1. 23
2. 8
3. 1
4. 7

Page 61
1. $20.00
2. 23 boxes
3. 75 students
4. Charles 40 cards
   Minh 40 cards